Suicide

Teen Suicide Prevention

Written By

Acie Cargill

Synopsis

So your teenage child is exhibiting symptoms of depression. You know there is something wrong. He or she used to seem perfectly normal. Full of life. Happy to be alive. Sure there were moments when emotions might flare up. That is part being a person. We might be more emotionally involved than necessary and sometimes we get carried away. Everybody does sometimes. Or at least they used to. Maybe they have outgrown the intensity of strong emotions and everything has been fairly mild and calm for years now.

But we are talking about teenagers. Hormones acting upon them and causing feelings that they might not understand and might not be able to control. Human maturation takes such a long time. So many years we spend in our childhood and that includes as teenagers. They read all kinds of stuff in books and watch television. All kinds of stuff. And movies and of course, the internet. A myriad of a variety of programming they are exposed to. Other generations didn't have to deal with all that.

I think parents should discuss everything with their teenager. All the stuff they read and watch. The ideas and experiences they see and read about. Talk about it with them. Don't make them take in inside and go secret with all their thoughts. You have to keep an open mind. It is up to you to accept your child's interests and attempts at personal learning. You can't be domineering when the child is sharing their real thoughts with you. If they are old enough to think for themselves then they are old enough for you to respect their rights as a person. Just like you expect to be respected.

About the Author

Acie Cargill is a poet, a songwriter, and a prose writer. He studied poetry with USA Poet Laureate Mark Strand and Illinois Poet Laureate Gwendolyn Brooks. He studied novel writing with Thomas Berger, who wrote Little Big Man (that Arthur Penn made into a movie with Dustin Hoffman in the lead role). Cargill also studied journalism with instructor Jean Daily. His work is a synthesis of all these styles.

He is a member of American Mensa and formerly Edited the Mensa Journal of Poetry. He also is a member of the Grammy Association, and The US Quill and Scroll Society.

Cargill is a vegetarian, a former holistic physician, a musical performer on a variety of instruments, an environmental activist, a lecturer, medical reviewer, a lover, and a seer.

Website

http://aciecargill.com

Contact

aciecargill@gmail.com

Other Books Written by the Author:

Puerto Rico

Aberrations

Chronicles

Terrorism

Modern Love

Ends and odds

Illiana: The Border Area Between Illinois and Indiana

Pullman

Che and Fidel - A Reading Play of the Cuban Revolution

Celia Sanchez - A Play of the Cuban Revolution

Paschke - A Play

Gwendolyn Brooks: A Play

Rasputin - A Play

Nietzsche - A Play

Bob Dylan, The Early Years - A Musical Play

Michael Jackson - A Play

Einstein - A Biographical Play

El Chapo - A Play In 3 Acts

Raisins and Roaches - A Three Month Diary of a Crack Addict

Susan B. Anthony - A Biographical Play

Kankakee

Harriet Tubman - A Biographical Play

Tesla - A Biographical Play

Vegan Saint - A Play in 3 Acts

Martin Luther King, Jr - A Play

Great Migration: A Play in 3 Acts

George Pullman - A Play in Three Acts

Frederick Douglass - A Biographical Play

Freud - A Biographical Play in 3 Acts

The Underground Railroad - An Educational Play

Payton, Jordan, Ali - A Biographical Play

Mr. Nobody - A Play

The Kid From Left Field - A Play

Puerto Rico, A Dream of Independence - A Play in 3 Acts

Crack Madness - A Monologue Play

Johnny Appleseed - A Family Play

Dr. Jekll and Mr. Hyde - A Modernized Play

Obama - Obama - A Play In 3 Acts

Will Rogers - A Biographical Monologue

Merle Haggard - A Biographical Monologue

Mother Teresa - A Biographical Monologue

Gwendolyn Brooks - A Biographical Monologue

Love Life of Susan B. Anthony - A Monologue Play

Sojourner Truth - A Biographical Monologue plus Narrator

Harriet Tubman and The Underground Railroad - A Play

Helen Keller, Words and Wisdom - A Biographical Play

Eugene Debs and the 1894 Pullman Strike - A Play

The Rising - A Play

Walt Disney - A Biographical One Act Play

The Experiments of Dr. Victor Frankenstein - A Play - Based on the novel by Mary Shelley

Karl Marx - A One Act Play

Martin Luther at The Diet of Worms - A One Act Play

Martin Luther King: Monologue and Narrator Play

Frederick Douglass - Monologue and Narrator Play

Kaepernick - A One Act Play

Settling South Holland - A Play In 2 Acts

Kaepernick - A Full-Length Play

My Son Died From An Overdose - A Play

Overdose - A One Act Play

Always a Marine First

Erotic Muslim Polygamy

George Dolton's Bridge to Freedom Underground Railroad - A One-Act Play

Greta Thunberg - A One-Act Play About Climate Change

A Brief History of the Philippines

Goat With No Horns - Voodoo Cannibals in Haiti

Johnny Cash - Monologue Play

Muhammad Words Of Wisdom

Jesus Words Of Wisdom

Bob Hope - Biographical Monologue

The Cargills of Graves County, Ky

Keith Raniere and the NXIVM Sex Club

Words of Wisdom – Native Americans, Ancient Greeks, Buddha and African-Americans

Words of Wisdom – Mark Twain, Benjamin Franklin, Shakespeare and Solomon

The Trial of Eddie Gallagher, Navy SEAL

Climate Crisis - A Plan to Prevent Future Flooding

Yukio Mishima - Life, Death, Hara Kiri

My "Cuzin Willie" Nelson - A Biographical Monologue

The World's Most Amazing Person, Elon Musk

The Beatles: Early Years - A One-Act Play

Red Summer Race Riot Chicago 1919 - Eyewitnesses John Harris and Ida B. Wells

Jeffrey Epstein - Illicit Kicks and Retribution

Gandhi - A Brief Biography

Jeffrey Epstein - Death Controversy

Greta Thunberg - Coming to America

Jeffrey Epstein Honeypots - Wealth, Women, and Girls

Tom Dreesen - Monologue Play

Roswell 1947

Greta Thunberg - How Dare You!

Table of Contents

1. Introduction

More young people commit suicide under the age of 18 than in the 18-24 age bracket. And the main cause seems to be depression. So what is that all about? Younger people are more depressed? When they are usually in great health and vitality and have the most to look forward to. It just doesn't make sense for them to suffer from depression that is so severe that they would even consider doing suicide. But a lot of teenagers do and a lot of them actually attempt it and sometimes they are successful at it.

Among teenage girls there is a high correlation between eating disorders and thoughts of suicide. Anorexia Nervosa. Bulimia. Over-eating. Junk eating. Just in general the person is probably suffering from some kind of obsessive-compulsive disorder and it often relates to food. Compulsive eating or compulsive not eating and an obsession with food. Often the person is depressed and has to be watched carefully and hopefully given some kind of beneficial therapy.

It is a fine line between providing beneficial counselling and driving the person deeper into their unhealthy personal ideas. It is not easy to work with any unbalanced person, but especially a teenager whose mind and personality is just developing. Going from childhood to adulthood. A time of transition. Misunderstandings. Excessive sensitivities because the person's feelings are just emerging and have not been jaded.

Problems with their parents are common. In fact, the majority of teenagers who have considered suicide claim that their parents do not understand them, whether they are incapable of understanding them or just not interested. At least, in the teenager's opinion. Dissension between the parents is disturbing to the teenager. They like peace between their parents. No arguing, no separations, and definitely no divorces. Parents of teenagers have to stick it out and make every effort to provide emotional security for the teen. Forget your own feelings and perceived importance. What is really important is that you have a developing teenager who is watching and listening to everything you do.

Do you want to drive your child into a state of depression? It is a mental illness which is not easy to relieve and can get progressively worse. Complications. Emotional difficulties cannot always be blamed on the parents, but quite often they can be. As a parent, you might not even think that your teenage child even cares about you one way or another. They might seem disinterested in their parents, but they do care. You are the most important people to them. More than their own friends. Or really anybody else. They might not express it, but you are constantly in the back of their minds. You are always there, even if it seems they don't care.

Your goal should be to raise mentally healthy teenagers who are going to grow into productive well-adjusted adults. That is what being a parent is all about. That is more important than any of your person wants. There is really nothing else you need more than taking care of your kids. Show them attention and love and listen to what they say and watch what they do. They need your attention and your approval. It might not seem like it, but it is the most important thing in their young lives.

You sure don't want to lose them. Your kids are the most important things that you have. You know that. Sometimes you just get distracted and put your own whims above theirs. Show some interest in their lives. Make them feel that their lives have value to you. It really does matter and makes a difference to them. For their emotional health.

2. Teen Suicides

Suicide is the third leading cause of death in young people ages 15 to 24. Boys are 4 times more likely to die from suicide than girls. Girls are more likely to try to commit suicide than boys. Guns are used in more than half of all youth suicides.

The teen years are a stressful time. They are filled with major changes. These include body changes, changes in thoughts, and changes in feelings. Strong feelings of stress, confusion, fear, and doubt may affect a teen's problem-solving and decision-making. He or she may also feel a pressure to succeed.

For some teens, normal developmental changes can be very unsettling when combined with other events, such as changes in their families, such as divorce, siblings moving out, or moving to a new town. Changes in friendships. Problems in school. Other losses. These problems may seem too hard or embarrassing to overcome. For some, suicide may seem like a solution.

Risk factors are one or more mental or substance abuse problems, impulsive behaviors, undesirable life events such as being bullied or recent losses, such as the death of a parent, family history of mental or substance abuse problems, family history of suicide, family violence, including physical, sexual, or verbal or emotional abuse, past suicide attempts, gun in the home, imprisonment, and exposure to the suicidal behavior of others, such as from family or peers, in the news, or in fiction stories.

Many of the warning signs of suicide are also symptoms of depression. They are changes in eating and sleeping habits, loss of interest in normal activities, withdrawal from friends and family members, acting-out behaviors and running away, alcohol and drug use, neglecting one's personal appearance, unnecessary risk-taking, obsession with death and dying, more physical complaints often linked to emotional distress, such as stomachaches, headaches, and extreme tiredness, ,loss of interest in school or schoolwork, feeling bored, problems focusing, feeling he or she wants to die, lack of response to praise, another warning sign is making plans or efforts toward committing suicide, says "I want to kill myself," or "I'm going to commit suicide," gives verbal hints, such as "I won't be a problem much longer," or "If anything happens to me, I want you to know ...." gives away favorite things or throws away important belongings, becomes suddenly cheerful after being depressed, may express strange thoughts, writes one or more suicide notes. These warning signs may seem like other health problems. Have your teen see his or her healthcare provider for a diagnosis.

3. Sexual consequences

You must have expected that sex would be a factor. How about sexual abuse. Occasionally a boy is abused by his mother, but usually it is the father abusing his daughter. It might seem like not much of a big deal to him. Just lust. A kick lasting for a short time. It is possible that the incest. is more of a big deal to her. Probably the sex act itself was not especially memorable. It happens and then it is over.

A factor that might not have been considered by the father is the loss of trust and the loss of respect, maybe even the loss of love that the daughter had for her father. Can things ever be the same between them again? That is doubtful. They have broken an unwritten rule and they both know that it was wrong. Nobody has to tell them. They just know. There are some morality lessons that just come naturally. Not necessarily a stated offense, but they both know it. Especially the girl.

She feels violated by her own father and it is not something she will ever forget.

Probably it felt good at least to the guy and was exciting somehow and they will do it again as the opportunity arises. Males get aroused. Get satisfied and their minds go some other subject. The daughter tries to make sense of what happened or is happening. The feelings and thoughts do not go away. It is in her mind. She knows something is wrong. She begins to blame herself. What did she do to bring it on? Was she just being affectionate? And somehow it became interpreted as sexual to her father or brother. The sex act is an abuse of her love. She knows she feels guilty, but she doesn't understand exactly why. She is not to blame, but she thinks she is.

I don't think an episode of incest or occasional episodes is a strong enough impetus to make a girl want to kill herself. It is a contributing factor. Adds to her tendency to becoming depressed. Other things will happen to make it worse, but the incest may be the event that opened a door in her psyche that leads to depression. It is a start. The beginning of the end? The end of her joyous girlhood. She can still be happy, but maybe not as completely as before.

There will be changes in her. She will look at things differently than she did. At least a little bit differently. Probably not in an especially beneficial way. Hopefully she can put the event behind her for the most part. If she resisted and there was a violent incestuous rape, then certainly the lasting effects will be more profound and more difficult to recover from.

Many girls do resist any sexual advances from their father or brother or even a sister. They resist and sometimes report the person to an authority, especially if the perpetrator is persistent. Probably there will be some lasting effects from this encounter also. Even if there was no physicality. Sexuality is something girls, and later as women, have to learn to deal with and most of them do. They don't understand it. Why is this happening? It has not been part of her life. Why now?

All of us are different from everybody else. We have a lot of similarities, but not exact. Things us affect us all differently. Sometimes the same event will barely be noticed by one girl, but that event can be severely disruptive to another. Some girls are just more delicate. More sensitive to their surroundings and more sensitive to everything that happens to them. Some girls can just laugh a lot of things off. Life is fun. Keep it that way. Enjoy life as it comes. Other girls can't seem to do that. Something may affect them in a way that they develop an eating disorder. Or a sleep disorder. Or a concentration disorder. Or a co-ordination disorder. There are so many possibilities.

Men should consider all the possibilities that their action may result in, but they don't. Sexuality can be so dominant in some men. Even if it is perverted. Even if it is unwelcome. Guys can't seem to control themselves sometimes. Even if they a re well controlled most of the time, they can lose their self- control occasionally. Sexuality is a strong driving force in males. For a variety of reasons. Physical reasons that result in a powerful physical drive for sex. And when they are under the control of the sex demon, they usually don't stop to consider all the consequences.

Females are stronger emotionally than guys. Females have a wider range of emotions and are more expressive of those emotions. More joy, more sorrow, more love, more hatred. Tears, elation. Trying to understand everything that happens. Everything has to fit in a compartment. Be classified. Incest doesn't fit in any of the right places and the girl begins to deal with unhappiness that can never leave completely. This residual effect if the beginning of depression.

4. Associates

Quite often the associations of teenagers are related to school. Large numbers of students are in the schools. Sometimes the students know a lot of other students and sometimes the students are fairly isolated and are basically solitary individuals. Even seemingly popular students might in actuality be alone most of the time. Many people adjust to being alone. They accept it and after a while, it doesn't bother them. They don't dwell on it. It is just them. Their life. Probably it is all they have ever known.

So are these loners more prone to become suicidal. Probably yes. More prone, but certainly not necessarily susceptible to suicide. There are thousands of teen suicides every year but that does not mean it is common. There are many millions of teenagers who have no thoughts or considerations of killing themselves. They might not be pleased with the way their lives are shaping up, but that is not enough reason to take their own lives.

Can a person be bullied into becoming suicidal? Probably yes. To an extent. But not exclusively. There are probably other factors that contribute to the persons susceptibility. How about a dissatisfaction with life in general? But we are dealing with teenagers, so their dissatisfaction hasn't been going on very long. Probably no more than a few years. To even consider suicide as an alternative, that unhappiness with their life must probably be combined with severe emotional depression. Maybe even an obsession with depression. Ending your life is a big deal. You can only do it once. Most people will consider other options. Other possibilities for staying alive.

Occasionally there are epidemics of teen suicides. One school in England had almost 30 students kill themselves. Usually by hanging. Each time the survivors made posts on social media about suicide victim with a lot of commentary and soon there would be another suicide. One after another. Sometimes several in a week. The students were all involved with the same websites and word got around a lot about each new death. A big moment of fame and notoriety,

Any factor in their lives may contribute to social isolation and criticism such as being gay, or overweight, or unattractive in some way, or maybe not very bright, maybe quiet, or from a poor background, not stylishly dressed, maybe not clean. Anything that will give individuals and groups a possible reason to talk about them. Sometimes openly and sometimes just among a group. Sometimes making fun of someone in a jovial way and sometimes with nastiness. Kids are not always very nice to other kids. Could be jealousy. Maybe the person just seems different. Nobody will want to be friends with the outcast because then they will become an outcast next. So the outcast is driven further into themselves.

Schools can be a like big beehives with students going about their lives in class and then during hallway breaks and lunchroom behavior. Some people seem to be in demand for socializing and some are not. Sometimes a person is tried out in a social whirl and is rejected and then ignored. Students can be overtly friendly, and also overtly unfriendly. Especially in groups.

So what can a rejected individual do? Trying to gain re-acceptance in a group will probably not work. Once you are rejected it is very hard to break the ice that forms. So, your choice is becoming an introvert or associating with other rejects. Everyone has value if you give them a chance inn your life. Let the snobs huddle together in their exclusive hatred. You can make friends with people who are possibly less socially desirable, but they may have more to offer in their friendship than the snobs.

Introverts also can have good lives. They must learn to accept who they are and take pride in the attributes that makes them separate. It is a step in their maturation. Acceptance of who they are. Not trying to be who they are not. Not needing attention. That is important. You must accept who you are. That is the most important thing. Your own personal appreciation of who you are. Accepting and not being ashamed or sorry in any way.

Dwelling on your singularity and being alone can cause early stages of becoming depressive. Your life may start to seem unimportant and maybe even not worthwhile. Do you need therapy? Maybe, or how about meditation? Like a therapeutic meditation. Self-improvement and self-appreciation. Lessen the importance as to what others think of you. Explore your inner self and enjoy the qualities that make you different. Not ashamed of them. Appreciate who you are and be joyful that you are who you are.

Don't be concerned about anybody else's opinion about anything about you. You are the most important. Your opinion is the one that counts. They don't really even know you. Just forget any other opinions. They are meaningless. Your life is valuable. You are unique. The product of a billion years of slow evolution. Don't waste it. Live your life fully and for as long as you can. Live love. Share the love.

5. Depression

Depression is a mental health disorder characterized by persistently depressed mood and loss of interest in activities, causing significant impairment in daily life. The person might dwell on their personal problems instead of doing anything to alleviate them and sink further into depression. Like a cycle becoming a whirlpool of despair.

The person has little interest or pleasure in doing things that formerly they enjoyed. It can lead to a feeling of hopelessness. Sleep disorders, trouble falling asleep and staying asleep. Can result in too much sleeping. Lethargic with very little energy. Poor appetite or overeating. Severe weight loss or weight gain. Person feels they are a failure in everything they do and don't even want to try things. Can't concentrate or make decisions. Talking or moving slowly or it can be expressed by restlessness. Thoughts that you are better off dead. Suicidal thoughts.

Today people commonly take antidepressant medications, but those antidepressants may increase suicidal thoughts or actions in some teens within the first few months of treatment or when the dose is changed. Depression and other serious mental illnesses are the most important causes of suicidal thoughts or actions. People who have or have a family history of bipolar illness, or suicidal thoughts or actions may have a particularly high risk. Pay close attention to any changes, especially sudden changes in mood, behavior, thoughts or feelings, especially symptoms such as anxiety, irritability, impulsivity, trouble sleeping, aggressive behavior or suicidal thoughts.

Depression affects how you feel, think, and handle daily activities, such as sleeping, eating, or working. To be diagnosed with depression, the symptoms must be present for at least two weeks. Some forms of depression are slightly different, or they may develop under unique circumstances.

Persistent depressive disorder (also called dysthymia) is a depressed mood that lasts for at least two years. A person diagnosed with persistent depressive disorder may have episodes of major depression along with periods of less severe symptoms, but symptoms must last for two years to be considered persistent depressive disorder.

Psychotic depression occurs when a person has severe depression plus some form of psychosis, such as having disturbing false fixed beliefs called delusions or hearing or seeing upsetting things that others cannot hear or see, hallucinations. The psychotic symptoms typically have a depressive "theme," such as delusions of guilt, poverty, or illness.

Seasonal affective disorder is characterized by the onset of depression during the winter months, when there is less natural sunlight. This depression generally lifts during spring and summer. Winter depression, typically accompanied by social withdrawal, increased sleep, and weight gain, predictably returns every year in seasonal affective disorder.

Bipolar disorder is different from depression, but it is included in this list is because someone with bipolar disorder experiences episodes of extremely low moods that meet the criteria for major depression (called "bipolar depression"). But a person with bipolar disorder also experiences extreme high – euphoric or irritable – moods called "mania".

If you have been experiencing some of the following signs and symptoms most of the day, nearly every day, for at least two weeks, you may be suffering from depression:

Persistent sad, anxious, or "empty" mood

Feelings of hopelessness, or pessimism

Irritability

Feelings of guilt, worthlessness, or helplessness

Loss of interest or pleasure in hobbies and activities

Decreased energy or fatigue

Moving or talking more slowly

Feeling restless or having trouble sitting still

Difficulty concentrating, remembering, or making decisions

Difficulty sleeping, early-morning awakening, or oversleeping

Appetite and/or weight changes

Thoughts of death or suicide, or suicide attempts

Aches or pains, headaches, cramps, or digestive problems without a clear physical cause and/or that do not ease even with treatment

Not everyone who is depressed experiences every symptom. Some people experience only a few symptoms while others may experience many. Several persistent symptoms in addition to low mood are required for a diagnosis of major depression.

Depression is one of the most common mental disorders in the U.S. Current research suggests that depression is caused by a combination of genetic, biological, environmental, and psychological factors.

Depression can happen at any age, but often begins in adulthood.

Depression is now recognized as occurring in children and adolescents, although it sometimes presents with more prominent irritability than low mood. Many chronic mood and anxiety disorders begin as high levels of anxiety.

Risk factors include:

Personal or family history of depression

Major life changes, trauma, or stress

Certain physical illnesses and medications

Depression, even the most severe cases, can be treated. The earlier that treatment can begin, the more effective it is.

Depression is usually treated with medications, psychotherapy, or a combination of the two.

No two people are affected the same way by depression and there is no "one-size-fits-all" for treatment. It may take some trial and error to find the treatment that works best for you.

Antidepressants are medicines that treat depression. They may help improve the way your brain uses certain chemicals that control mood or stress. You may need to try several different antidepressant medicines before finding the one that improves your symptoms and has manageable side effects. A medication that has helped you or a close family member in the past will often be considered.

Antidepressants take time – usually 2 to 4 weeks – to work, and often, symptoms such as sleep, appetite, and concentration problems improve before mood lifts, so it is important to give medication a chance before reaching a conclusion about its effectiveness. If you begin taking antidepressants, do not stop taking them without the help of a doctor. Sometimes people taking antidepressants feel better and then stop taking the medication on their own, and the depression returns. When you and your doctor have decided it is time to stop the medication, usually after a course of 6 to 12 months, the doctor will help you slowly and safely decrease your dose. Stopping them abruptly can cause withdrawal symptoms.

6. Teen suicide intervention and prevention

Young people who feel connected, supported and understood are less likely to commit suicide. Connectedness, a sense of being supported and respected, are protective factors for young people at risk of suicide. For some reason kids today are experiencing more pressure. Intervention issues for communities to address include: suicide contagion, developmental understanding of suicide, development and suicide risk, and the influence of culture

One can help prevent adolescent suicide by discouraging isolation, addressing a child's depression which is correlated with suicide, getting rid of any objects that a child could use to commit suicide, and simply paying attention to what the child does or feels.

Schools are a great place to provide more education and support on suicide prevention. Since students spend a majority of their time at school, school can be either a haven from or a source of suicidal triggers, and students' peers can heavily influence their state of mind. The school setting is an ideal environment to educate students on suicide and have support readily available.

Threats of suicide are a cry for help. Always take such statements, thoughts, behaviors, or plans very seriously. Any teen who expresses thoughts of suicide should not be left alone and should be evaluated right away. Talk with your teen's healthcare provider about suicide and have a written emergency plan.

Any teen who has tried to commit suicide needs a physical checkup first to rule out life-threatening health problems. He or she should then get a mental health evaluation and treatment until he or she is stable. This often will take place at an inpatient facility to make sure of the child's safety.

Treatment will depend on your child's symptoms, age, and general health. It will also depend on how severe the condition is.

Treatment starts with a detailed evaluation of events in your teen's life during the 2 to 3 days before the suicidal behaviors. Treatment may include individual therapy, family therapy. parents play a vital role in treatment. An extended hospital stay, if needed. This gives the child a supervised and safe environment.

Learning the warning signs of teen suicide can prevent an attempt. Keeping open communication with your teen and his or her friends gives you a chance to help when needed. Keep medicines and guns away from children and teens. Get your teen help for any mental or substance abuse problems. Support your teen. Listen, try not to offer undue criticism, and stay connected.

7. Home teenage suicide prevention

So your teenage child is exhibiting symptoms of depression. You know there is something wrong. He or she used to seem perfectly normal. Full of life. Happy to be alive. Sure there were moments when emotions might flare up. That is part being a person. We might be more emotionally involved than necessary and sometimes we get carried away. Everybody does sometimes. Or at least they used to. Maybe they have outgrown the intensity of strong emotions and everything has been fairly mild and calm for years now.

But we are talking about teenagers. Hormones acting upon them and causing feelings that they might not understand and might not be able to control. Human maturation takes such a long time. So many years we spend in our childhood and that includes as teenagers. They read all kinds of stuff in books and watch television. All kinds of stuff. And movies and of course, the internet. A myriad of a variety of programming they are exposed to. Other generations didn't have to deal with all that.

I think parents should discuss everything with their teenager. All the stuff they read and watch. The ideas and experiences they see and read about. Talk about it with them. Don't make them take in inside and go secret with all their thoughts. You have to keep an open mind. It is up to you to accept your child's interests and attempts at personal learning. You can't be domineering when the child is sharing their real thoughts with you. If they are old enough to think for themselves then they are old enough for you to respect their rights as a person. Just like you expect to be respected.

So you have to expand your role from parent to also being a friend with the teenager. A friend that gives encouragement and understanding. Not critical. Ease up on the teenager and you may have to accept a lot of things that you don't understand or approve of. You want your teenager to be able to speak to you about any subject and know that you will be an open-minded listener. You don't want to just be a milk toast parent that lets the teenager bully you by using the threat of suicide to control you. That's no good either. The idea is for you to be an important part of the teenager's personal emotional support system

You naturally have things you believe in that may be in conflict with something your teenager believes in. The idea here is to not be an overbearing parent. Your goal is to be a friend and agree with what your teenager has to say and try to understand. Even if you vehemently disagree. You cannot express that vehemence to the child. Talk about it. Tell him or her that you understand, but it is not in conjunction with the way you were brought up. It doesn't mean there is no middle ground. Talk about it and try to work out your differences in a friend to friend way. Be happy that you are communicating. That is very important.

Suicide is not the only thing that can go wrong when there is no communication between the teenager and the parent.

Eating disorders are becoming more prevalent. Drug addiction. Especially opioids can lead to overdose death. Becoming promiscuous with possible pregnancy or disease. Generalized anti-social behavior even to the point of criminality. There's a lot of things that can go wrong with your teenager. It doesn't mean that it will. But it might.

So are the parents to blame for the child's behavioral difficulties? Nothing is all the time, of course. But the parent's relationship with the teenager, and before that with the child, is very influential in that person's development. Naturally there are going to be social influences at school and on the streets for the teenager growing up. Every kid gets exposed to all kinds of experiences and emotional exposures. Every kid. Most of them are able to just deal with it and go on to other people and places. Some are disturbed profoundly and need your help to avoid becoming mentally ill. And yes, depression is a mental illness.

Those are the teenagers that I am concerned about. They are broken. Injured. But not hopeless. They can be cared for and brought back to normalcy and live a fine life with no exceptional problems. It is up to the parent to save the day. A teacher might help or a counsellor or even a well-balanced friend. They can all help, but the cure for the mentally ill teenager is the parent. Take the time. Change your attitude. Bring the teenager back to the surface from the depths. Normalcy again. It can be done.

It is going to take heart to heart talks. A lot of them. Some of the problems causing the mental illness may go back a long time. They need to be brought out and discussed. The teen must understand that you didn't intentionally mean to cause harm, but it was your own weakness that led to the mistakes. Human frailty. Apologize. Beg forgiveness. If the teen forgives you then maybe it will be forgotten. Talk about all the things that are bothering him or her. Really talk about it. Be a good listener. You are not a judge and you are not on trial. You are learning and asking forgiveness.

Clean the air. It is stagnant and causing your child to be sick. It doesn't just happen by itself. You did it. It is time for you to undo it. You must be a bigger person yourself and save your child by being his or her friend. This is a crisis. The teenager may die or at least be impeded from living a normal, joyous life. It is the greatest cause you could possibly do in your life is to save your child's life by being understanding and approving. Bring him or her back to a full happy life again. Lift the depression off. You are probably the only person who can. And be patient. It will take a while.